Introduction

War and the conduct of war, is a fundamental, moral, human endeavor that is based on ultimate questions. Western thought processes about this endeavor have grown along a strain of thinking called the Just War Tradition (JWT). Justice is the determiner of whether or not a given activity is right or wrong. Just War thinking primarily focuses on responses to attack, rather than on first actions. It is the first actions that are under scrutiny here. The dilemma is whether or not the pursuit of justice can include the first use of military might. The Just War Tradition provides the moral framework for preemptive acts.

Operation Iraqi Freedom (OIF) posed the first real dilemma for the United States in the immediate aftermath of the events of September 11, 2001. The reason OIF offered the opportunity to question the actions of the United States in its "War on Terror" is that some have called it a "preemptive war." If OIF was, or is, a preemptive war, it seems that it is a departure for the United States in its military thinking because the US has tended to enter conflict only after significant provocation, or at the request of other nations.

The first questioning of OIF focused on President George Bush's "new" thinking, which was to *preemptively* enter the sovereign borders of Iraq. Some said he was doing it "for the oil." Others said he was trying to "finish his father's unfinished business." Occasionally, the debate over OIF focused on whether it was the "right" thing to do, with many concluding it was the "wrong" thing to do for any number of reasons, including casualties, cost, and others. Relatively few people opposed the commencement of OIF. Those few who did oppose it argued that there was no self-defensive aspect to the operation—which is an appeal to Just War thinking.

Currently, the public debate has focused on "how the war was conducted,"[1] rather than on whether or not it was a right war. If the debate were to focus on the *rightness* or *wrongness* of the operation, it would be an appeal to Just War thinking. If the debate concentrated on how it was conducted, it would be a study in tactics, possibly in operational art.

The Western world needs to know if its thinking about Just War applies to the world today. The "world today" is in a state of confusion about how to think and what to do about extremists, jihadists, terrorists, rogue states and non-state actors. It needs to know if justice is achievable and if its long history of Just War thinking is applicable in dealing with these threats.

The Just War Tradition does illumine preemptive actions, including preemptive war. It does more than shed light on the subject; it dictates how preemptive actions should be undertaken.

Section 1

The Foundation of the Just War Tradition

The Just War Tradition has grown out of the interaction of states over the course of history. The threads of the JWT are usually connected back to Saint Ambrose and Saint Augustine. However, this is an inaccurate beginning point, as they were Christian Church Fathers, and as such, were the bearers of much responsibility in the connection of pre-Christ teaching with post-Christ teaching. Therefore, the JWT offers one chord in the continuous development and maturation of the thinking of a particular religious heritage. To the extent that any western political leaders follow the JWT, it is because the religious heritage has had an impact on political thinking.

The JWT bears up under scrutiny because "the light of human reason" follows it. It is not that the religious tradition is subservient to the rigor of logical thought, but because logical thought is illumined by the Judeo-Christian heritage of western nations.

There are significant failings in the adherence of nations to the JWT. These failings are often cited as examples of how the JWT does not carry the force of law or of moral imperative, such that political aims of nations override the limitations that the JWT would impose on the commencement, pursuit, and cessation of conflict.

Throughout this thesis, the term *nation* will be used as a generic term in place of several words which merit their own study: nation, state, nation-state, Wesphalian state, country. The scope of this thesis precludes an evaluation of what constitutes a nation or a state. It will be used to identify broad political categories of disparate groupings based on ethnicity, language, religion, geography, and borders (as they are currently drawn, whether accurately or not). There is even some applicability to "non-state" actors. So-called non-state actors, in some cases, employ weapon systems and engage in warfare, ensuring their inclusion in the dialogue of international action, including the use of force against them.

It is not required that political leadership be either Jewish or Christian to adhere to the JWT. When the argumentation about a nation's military actions follows the categories of the JWT, then the tradition has weight even if its criteria are not formalized in law. Also, it is common in the human experience that individuals, groups, and governments try to interpret any law to their own advantage. In the hypothetical situation that any nation were to pass into law the parts of the JWT as its criteria for entering conflict, it is possible that it would later interpret its own codification to allow it to enter a war that seemed expedient to it. Whether it is legislated or not, the JWT has had a significant impact on the thinking of western nations, such that many of its parts influence the debates over the use of force, and much of it has been captured in various codes, conventions, and agreements.

The Geneva Conventions and the Hague Conventions have formalized many parts of the JWT, especially detailing the conduct of the participants in a war. These conventions now have the force of international law, as 194 countries are signatories to the agreements.[2]

There are two parts of the JWT. The first part is concerned with the justice of going to war—*Jus ad Bellum*. The second part is concerned with the justice of the behavior of the parties once they have begun to fight with each other—*Jus in Bello*. Sometimes a third part, dealing with the aftermath of war—*Jus post Bello*—is discussed, but is not central to this study.

Jus ad Bellum

1. Just Cause

The reasons for engaging in war must be proper. This is an appeal to justice, as is all of the Just War Tradition. Within the JWT, every aspect is about justice. In this case, there must be a just reason for beginning the conflict of arms. The reasons usually given are: 1. Self-defense, including that of a weaker neighbor;[3] 2. Redress a Wrong; 3. Indemnity.

> The justifiable causes generally assigned for war are three, defence, indemnity, and punishment...it is right to defend, to recover, and the encroachment on which it is right to punish. There is an omission in this enumeration, unless the word recover be taken in its most extensive sense. For recovering by war what we have lost, includes indemnity for the past, as well as the prosecution of our claim to a debt.[4]

Many commentators leave out *indemnity*, though Grotius includes it as its own category. He does so because it has enough substance to be treated as a separate grouping. It may be permissible to put it under the heading of redressing a wrong; however, the commentators who leave it out do not deal with it once it has been grouped into another category. This is certainly because it is difficult—possibly opening the door to touchy subjects, such as going to war for no apparent reason of violence committed, but simply to arbitrate an indemnity.

Self-defense is the most easily defined category for just cause. Hence, the United Nations Charter recognizes it and allows self-defense against acts of aggression without UN Security Council approval.[5] Other cases would require approval by the council. Other UN categories allow for defending weaker neighbors and redressing wrongs, including the difficult cases of "peacekeeping" and "peacemaking."[6]

2. Right Authority

The legitimate authority of a government must enact war. Many commentators say, "a formal declaration of war."[7] The important element of this is that a government inform opponents and friends alike, that it intends to enter armed conflict.[8] Some commentators would also require a series of notifications leading up to the formal declaration.[9] Additionally, international recognition of the responsibility of an attacking party to give warning is formalized in the Hague Conventions.[10]

The current enigma that is the United States declaration of war process does not infringe on this principle. Because the democracy of the US is built on a separation of powers basis, with its bicameral legislative branch, there is political gamesmanship over who officially enacts the war. But the loud and obvious process, on the world stage is such that there can be no surprise and that numerous notifications are made prior to the Commander in Chief ordering the beginning of violence. This, in effect, is the legitimate declaration of war.

3. Right Intention

Right intention requires a nation to intend by its war only that which is necessary and not to use its greater capabilities to advance its own selfish interests.[11] This means that even a corporate body as large as a nation ought to desire only that which is good. This means that it should seek the betterment of not simply itself, but all its neighbors. Its purpose is to correct some wrong and to achieve some protection while avoiding the prohibited intents of "vindictive anger and malicious revenge."[12]

4. Proportionality of Ends

The violence of the war entered by the wronged party must be proportional to the injury that was suffered at the outset. Thus, nations are prohibited from using force greater than that required to redress the injury suffered. Furthermore, once the just proportion of the wrong has been met, the conflict is to be ended, such that the original wronged party does not begin to do wrong himself.[13]

5. Last Resort

The last resort category in the JWT dictates that all other means of resolving conflict have been exhausted. Most often this is interpreted to mean that all other diplomatic means have reached an impasse;[14] that sanctions have not had their desired effect; that other strategic communication has fallen on deaf ears.[15] This is simplistic because it requires that military action be necessarily at only one end of a continuum, and at its extreme end. At first glance, diplomacy may end (because it has failed) when war starts. Former Secretary of Defense Caspar Weinberger stated this idea too simply when he says, "The commitment of forces should be a last resort."[16] A more actionable definition of the term *last resort* is to say that "war [is] the only reasonable means to right the wrong"[17] because it expands last resort to permit the use of force at the time it would be most effective. This statement clarifies that there may be a situation in which military means are the only suitable venue for rectifying a situation, which links this criterion to just cause, which was previously discussed.

6. Reasonable Hope of Success

Reasonable hope of success mandates that pragmatic and prudent evaluations be exercised prior to engaging in war. This category requires that proper planning be conducted prior to conducting war; that proper resources will be allocated for the war; that proper collective determination exists to continue the conflict through its most difficult periods all the way to its conclusion, once the choice for armed conflict has been made.[18] Retired General and former Secretary of State Colin Powell enumerated several considerations that ought to govern the choice to go to war.[19]

Reasonable hope of success deliberates whether or not it is expedient to undertake a conflict. Grotius argues that there are certain injustices that are tolerable if war is the only alternative. These may be minor injustices for which recourse to war is not worthwhile or relatively major injustices if any attempt to rectify them would result in failure.[20]

Furthermore, citizens' lives are not to be squandered. Death for a hopeless cause is not justifiable.[21] If the actions of the nation are governed by justice, the death of citizens for a hopeless cause is as repugnant as whatever wrong is to be corrected.

7. The Purpose is to Restore Peace

The peace post-conflict is supposed to be preferable to the conditions prior to conflict. The goal of any conflict must be "to attain or restore a just and durable peace."[22] Any other goal puts the conflict back into the category of *unjust*. Ceasefires can actually be counter-productive because they can set the conditions for a resumption of more intense hostilities. Therefore, even a cessation of hostilities is supposed to have the purpose of a better peace.[23]

Jus in Bello

The essential elements of *jus in bello* are: 1. Discrimination; 2. Proportionality; and 3. Minimum Force. Additionally, some commentators add a fourth element—Necessity. That is, *jus in bello* is primarily concerned with the restraint or limitation on violence once it has been entered.[24]

The category of discrimination identifies people in the vicinity of the conflict as combatants and noncombatants. Within these two larger categories are subcategories.

Combatants are armies, militia and volunteer corps which have a commander, wear uniforms or an emblem, carry arms openly and honor the laws and customs of war. However, as soon as a combatant becomes too ill to fight, lays down his weapons, is captured, or is otherwise taken out of the conflict, he becomes a noncombatant. Both noncombatants and prisoners of war captured by the enemy have the same rights.[25]

Noncombatants are defined as those who are "taking no active part in the hostilities."[26] By this definition, most often it is women, children and the aged who are noncombatants. The overarching principle in the teaching about noncombatants is the "intention not to harm those who do not deserve it."[27]

Proportionality requires that the amount of damage done by the offended nation to the offending nation not be greater than the wrong that was originally committed. The corresponding analogy is that you do not chop off a hand when a flick on the wrist is sufficient to correct a wrong. Similarly, once engaged in combat, units and individuals are not supposed to kill indiscriminately; not to maim; not to torture; not to mutilate dead bodies.[28] It is evident that discrimination and proportionality are bound together.

The minimum force requirement is also very closely related to proportionality, but focuses more on the tactics involved in the war. The force utilized in achieving an objective is to be the minimum required, not the maximum available. There is often some discussion on this point, as significant force is available to the military practitioner. An example sometimes used is that it would be permissible to drop a 500-pound bomb on a spire from which a sniper has been having significant effect, not because the 500-pound bomb is equivalent to his 140-grain bullet, but because the bomb is the minimum force available to oust him from the position, from which he has had such an imposing effect.

Necessity is not a requirement given by all commentators, but it follows minimum force. To continue the above example, a commander ought to employ the 500-pound bomb against the sniper if it is a necessity. If he is able to maneuver his unit out of the effective range of the sniper with no negative impact to his unit or the one he is supporting, then he will not have to bomb the sniper.

The subject of necessity is a difficult one. For its use in the Jus in Bello arena, it will be called military necessity. Michael Walzer discusses *necessity* in his book Just and Unjust Wars in his analysis of the moral nature of war because, if something is a necessity, it is right to pursue it, and conversely, wrong not to pursue it,[29] which makes it *jus ad bellum* argument.

Laws and conventions add what is essentially another element—unnecessary suffering. A military force is prohibited from using arms or projectiles that cause unnecessary suffering. This follows logically from proportionality and minimum force, but specifically addresses the weapons used in war. Those weapons are allowed to kill, but are prohibited from not killing and leaving the soldier in extreme agony.[30]

Section 2

Comparison of Commentators on Just War

The modern era has brought some good commentators on the subject of Just War, and has provided them with opportunities to evaluate the material. This section will provide insight to some of them, and will illustrate the range of thinking on the JWT. None of the commentators evaluated here uses all of the seven categories that comprise the JWT given at the outset. There is a sufficient overlap in their material to guide the study of the tradition. Some of the key differences or illuminating points from them will be given here.

Jean Bethke Elshtain's book Just War Against Terror: The Burden of American Power in a Violent World is particularly written to discuss what the United States ought to do after the terrorist attacks in New York City in September 2001. Her interpretation of the historic perspective of what constitutes Just Cause is that a war is "a response to a specific instance of unjust aggression perpetrated against one's own people or an innocent third party, or fought for a just cause."[31]

Edward LeRoy Long's interpretation of Just Cause is that a "war can be just only if employed to defend a stable order, or morally preferable cause against threats of destruction or the rise of injustice."[32] All of these reasons for war in Elshtain and Long are self defensive in their thinking. This is the trajectory of *just cause* throughout history. Long additionally gives a sixth item in the list of what constitutes a Just War, but it is essentially a Jus in Bello category. He says, "The just war theory has also entailed selective immunity… particularly for noncombatants."[33]

Susan Niditch gives an evaluation of war from a very specific vantage point. She studied war in the Old Testament age of the Hebrew people in a book titled War in the Hebrew Bible.

She does not specifically analyze it using the lens of the JWT. But the assumption of the OT Hebrews was that they went to war on occasions, and for reasons that were prescribed, that is ordered, by Yahweh. As such, they had *just cause, right authority*, and *right intent*. There were limitations to their conflicts, but again they were inspired by God. One of her points is that these inspired situations formed the basis for the subsequent ages.[34]

Paul Ramsey essentially disposes of the Reasonable Hope aspect of the JWT because of the preponderance of emphasis placed upon the "principle of expediency" in the modern world.[35] "Calculation of the consequences may in any given instance be sufficient to prove that an act of justified warfare cannot effectively, and therefore should not, be undertaken; but this alone would never establish the rightfulness of such action as legitimate or permitted by love in the first place."[36] Additionally, Ramsey's alignment with the JWT categories is in his commentary on Augustine. His book, War and the Christian Conscience, is primarily concerned with whether or not we are capable of conducting a just war, when we have the capability of killing millions of people at one time with nuclear weapons.

This provides the opportunity to demonstrate how essential elements of the JWT can oppose and balance each other. The hypothetical situation arises in which a weapon capable of killing hundreds of thousands is unleashed on a city. Clearly, innocent civilians are targeted, which is contrary to the discrimination category. However, the legitimate authority ordered it, and arguably fewer numbers were killed in the single massive strike against non-combatants than would have been killed if the opposing militaries had continued to fight long, bitter campaigns against each other, which is an appeal to proportionality, right intention, and restoration of peace.[37]

Michael Walzer's <u>Just and Unjust Wars</u> is considered a very important work on the subject of Just War. It is an excellent volume. In it, he cites case studies to illustrate his points. One of his key points is that war has a distinct and compelling moral element.[38] He does not argue this from a desire to "do the right thing," but because of the inherently ultimate outcomes of war—people die. His greatest contribution to the dialogue about the JWT is his formulating reasons for preemptive war, all of which are self-defense arguments (and which will be discussed below).

Alexander F.C. Webster and Darrell Cole wrote <u>The Virtue of War: The Christian Answer to the Peace Movement</u>. It is a compelling book because their premise is that war is essential if it is done with the proper moral imperative. They do not specifically give the Just War reason of restoration of peace, but their supreme call for the warrior is to do right in the world by pursuing justice.[39] The aspect of their study that is very interesting is a connection of thinking on Just War between the Eastern Orthodox Churches, the Roman Catholic Church, and Protestant teachings.[40]

Former Secretary of Defense Caspar Weinberger added a term to the lexicon of the United States when he asked if the "Vital Interest" of the nation was at stake.[41] This does not necessarily fit into any of the standard categories of the JWT. However, it can significantly temper the other arguments of the tradition, because in a very compelling moral situation, one in which all other elements of *jus ad bellum* may lead a nation to war, the vital national interest could prevent it. On the other hand, arguing vital interest could make it seem like a good idea to go to war over resources or conveniences, which would be in opposition to the JWT.

The following table provides a visual representation of the arguments of the authors mentioned above. The numeralization simply marks the order the evaluation appears in the author's study. It does not necessarily mark the category a given author thinks is the most important. Some columns are marked with an "x". In these cases, the author discusses the points at widely separated places in their work, rather than in a linear fashion, thus ordering, or weighting their categories would serve no purpose.

SCORECARD	ELSHTAIN	LONG	NIDITCH	POWELL	RAMSEY	WALZER	WEBSTER	WEINBERGER
Just Cause	2	2	X		X	X	2	
Right Authority	1	4	X		X		1	
Right Intention	3	3	X		X		3	
Proportionality of Ends						X		
Last Resort	4	1		2		X	4	6
Reasonable Hope	5	5		1,3,4,5,6			5	2,3,4,5
Restoration of Peace					X	X		

Commentator Comparison Table

Section 3

The Modern American Doctrines

There is a strain of thinking in modern America about war that diverges from adherence to the JWT. It is very "Clausewitzian" in its focus and is based on his assessment that "war is…an act of violence meant to force the enemy to do our will."[42] Yet most arguments for war are based on a moral foundation. For example, the Founding Fathers of the United States argued, "We hold these truths to be self-evident…" and that King George III had violated his responsibilities requiring the redress of grievances.[43] President George W. Bush said, "…our cause is just."[44]

Many, though not all, of the conflicts the United States has been involved in were entered on grounds directly related to the JWT. The United States' typical point of entry has been after some significant act of provocation (just cause—self-defense and to redress a wrong). But since the end of the Cold War, there has apparently been an increase in the number of involvements in conflicts which were not started by an attack on the US.

During the closing years of the 20th Century, two significant additions were made to the US thought process about war and the use of military force. The additions were attempts by two men to publicly delineate their positions on the use of armed forces.

The Weinberger Doctrine

Secretary of Defense Weinberger gave a speech in 1984 which presented six "tests to be applied when we are weighing the use of U.S. combat forces abroad."[45]

> 1. The Vital Interest of the US (or its allies) must be at stake prior to committing forces.
> 2. If troops are committed, it must be wholeheartedly with the intention of winning.
> 3. If troops are committed, political and military objectives must be clearly defined.
> 4. Force "size, composition and disposition" must be actively assessed and managed.
> 5. Popular and Congressional support must be behind the effort.
> 6. The commitment of forces should be a last resort.[46]

The Powell Doctrine

General Colin L. Powell wrote an article in 1992 which asked the following questions:

> 1. Is the political objective we seek to achieve important, clearly defined and understood?
> 2. Have all other nonviolent policy means failed?
> 3. Will military force achieve the objective?
> 4. At what cost?
> 5. Have the gains and risks been analyzed?
> 6. How might the situation that we seek to alter, once it is altered by force, develop further and what might be the consequences?[47]

The General's questions are pointedly focused on the issue of last resort—that the decision to go war was only made after every other means at the disposal of the nation had been expended and failed. Once the decision for war had been made, he is then focused on being successful in war. Powell said, "The reason for our success is that in every instance we have carefully matched the use of military force to our political objectives."[48]

The Weinberger and Powell doctrines primarily fall into the Just War category of a "reasonable hope of success." This is not necessarily surprising and probably should not cause any concern, for they were both very high level members of and proponents for the Department of Defense, which put them in the organization that ought to be most concerned with the question, "Can we succeed, given the tasks we are being asked to accomplish?" If Clausewitz is right "that war is simply an extension of political intercourse,"[49] then it must be the military man who, at the last, at least asks, "Can I be successful?"

Section 4

Post 9-11 Additions

The connection between the September 11th attacks and the Taliban regime in Afghanistan was not patently obvious to the common citizen, but the case was made by the nation's leaders including the President. The administration insured the connection to the JWT. Therefore, the military response of the United States followed the principles of the JWT: the US was acting with a just cause because the attack was obviously unprovoked; the case was made that the Taliban government of Afghanistan was knowingly harboring the actual offenders; the war against the government of Afghanistan was conducted after numerous warnings; and the US guaranteed proportionality by obligating itself to cease hostilities after the Taliban was removed and/or they had delivered the perpetrators of the crime.

That some have said operation Iraqi freedom was a preemptive war was mentioned previously. During the lead-up to operation Iraqi freedom, every reason that was given was essentially a JWT argument. The President addressed the nation using typical JWT reasoning in October 2002.[50] As addressed in the earlier section about legitimate first strike when under imminent attack, this is more difficult to argue in the modern era of cross-continent and intercontinental missiles than in earlier ages of massed armies at borders. Yet, imminent attack remains a category within just war thinking that permits a first strike, and this argument was made in the case of Iraq.[51] Significantly, the JWT category of "restore a better peace" was used because the US would work with other nations *post bellum* to bring a just government to Iraq.[52]

It is apparent that Clausewitz' principle applies: "warfare will always be interspersed with greater or smaller periods of rest."[53] The First Gulf War, Operation Desert Fox, Operation Southern Watch, Operation Northern Watch, and United Nations weapons inspections all culminated in the commencement of Operation Iraqi Freedom as the continuation of a long term war.

The significant addition to the war reasoning of the United States was that of preemptive terminology. The argumentation that led to Operation Iraqi Freedom was based on JWT terminology and reasoning. That argument combined with Clausewitz' principle of an increase in hostilities could have provided sufficient explanation to elevate the conflict in Iraq. However, the Bush Administration did not stop there. The preemptive terminology that was added appeared in the National Security Strategy (NSS) of 2002. In the NSS, it states "the United States has long maintained that the option of preemptive actions to counter a sufficient threat to our national security... to forestall or prevent such hostile acts (attacks against our military forces or civilian population) by our adversaries, the United States will, if necessary, act preemptively."[54]

The NSS does several things that are worthwhile in light of the JWT. It challenges the world community to "adapt the concept of imminent threat to the capabilities and objectives of today's adversaries", which is an appeal to the JWT *just cause*. It argues for restraint in using preemptive justification, recognizing that some might use it for purposes of aggression. And it disavows using preemptive actions for emerging threats.[55]

The NSS brought a significant expansion of thinking on JWT to the world stage. The conjunction of the release of the NSS with the buildup for OIF gave credibility to the notion that the US was engaging in a preemptive war in Iraq. It is this author's contention that OIF was **not** a preemptive action rather, that it was the NSS of 2002 which actually caused the conclusion that OIF was a preemptive attack by the US. It is unclear if the world community has effectively debated the legitimate exercise of preemptive war.

Section 5

Preemptive Self-Defense

It ought to have been noticed this far in this thesis that, in general, Just War thinking is reactive, that is, it is a series of thought processes in response to the use of force by someone else. The NSS of 2002 notwithstanding, the issue of preemption is raised. Can it be acceptable to initiate a conflict against another sovereign nation without that nation having committed a wrong by attacking first?

The general category of self-defense is one that is often granted as a legitimate reason for striking back, and striking back is exactly the key when we are talking about self-defense. The analogy of being in a bar, not doing anything that would provoke an assault, and being "sucker punched" is just this sort of scenario. Most people would agree that the one who was punched is allowed to strike back to the extent that he ends the conflict.

The analogy is consistent even at the national level. When one nation strikes another nation, the struck nation is permitted to strike back. The idea of proportionality is one that dictates limits to the offended nation.[56] It must desist from its striking back once the wrong has been redressed, or those who committed the initial strike have been brought to justice. It obviously disallows the obliteration of an entire citizenry.

National self-defense that is executed in a preemptive fashion when an opposing army is built up at the border is relatively straightforward, though not quite as obvious as the previous example. Most people would still grant that there is a legitimate reason for striking preemptively in this case.

The difficulty with personal preemptive self-defense and with national preemptive self-defense is that the opponent can always argue that he was not actually intending to attack. This difficulty can be dealt with fairly simply by the account of two or three witnesses.[57] Back in the bar, the individual could preemptively punch his attacker if there was sufficient threat and witnesses could verify that the preemptive punch was legitimate. At the national level, coalition partners, international community recognition, or United Nations support can lend credibility in exactly the same way the witnesses do above. Thus, a nation, upon the counsel and agreement of its allies, could decide to preempt the apparent a threat of a gathering invasion.

An early attempt in the United States to define preemptive violence came from the Secretary of State Daniel Webster in the Caroline Case (1842) in which he wrote that in order to justify preemptive action "there must be shown 'a necessity of self-defense... instant, overwhelming, leaving no choice of means, and no moment for deliberation'."[58]

"Sufficient threat" is another way of answering the question as to whether or not the opponent was actually going to attack. This terminology means that once there is sufficient threat of invasion, the soon-to-be-attacked party may launch the first strike.

Michael Walzer tackles the issue of preemption in his work Just and Unjust Wars. But even his dealing with the issue is still essentially a self-defense argument. He says,

The line between legitimate and illegitimate first strikes is not going to be drawn at the point of imminent attack, but at the point of sufficient threat. That phrase is necessarily vague. I mean it to cover three things: a manifest intent to injure, a degree of active preparation that makes that intent a positive danger, and a general situation in which waiting, or doing anything other than fighting, greatly magnifies risk.[59]

Thus, in agreement with Walzer, the following principles permit a preemptive attack for the purpose of self-defense:

1. The aggressor has clearly demonstrated that it has the intent to injure.

2. The intent to injure poses a positive danger to another nation.

3. The threatened nation would greatly magnify its risk by not striking preemptively.

Section 6

Preemptive Actions

In the previous section the principles which permit a preemptive attack for the purpose of self-defense were established. In this section the right uses of preemption for purposes other than self-defense will be established. First strike when an army is at your border is understandable (maybe not quite as simple as striking back after being attacked, but nearly so). This is not necessarily a matter that is new to the modern world, however the modern era, with aircraft and missiles that can transit the globe in very short periods with absolutely no warning of a military buildup at a border, poses special difficulties.

The first thing to understand is the duty of the civil magistrate. The government of a nation must establish *tranquillitas ordinis*.[60] In order to establish ordinary tranquility, a government must provide for the security and protection of its citizens and those living inside its borders. These are precisely the tasks enumerated in the Preamble to the US Constitution:

-Establish Justice

-Insure Domestic Tranquility
-Provide for the Common Defense
-Promote the General Welfare
-Secure the Blessings of Liberty to ourselves and our posterity

Conclusion: Preemptive military action can be taken to protect and ensure the Tranquillitas Ordinis of a nation's own citizens.

The requirement of humankind to see to the protection of the weak or defenseless precedes the right of self-defense.[61] This means that endangering one's self on behalf of others is a responsibility that precedes the right to take self-preserving action. This applies to nations as well. There are many nations which adequately provide their citizens the conditions required of the civil magistrate, but which are incapable of defeating an attacking nation. In these cases, other strong nations ought to defend the weaker nation with the same passion they do for their own citizens.

Conclusion: Preemptive military action can be taken to protect and ensure the Tranquillitas Ordinis of the citizens of another nation.

If we accept the principle "We hold these truths to be self-evident, that all men are created equal, that they are endowed by their Creator with certain unalienable Rights, that among these are Life, Liberty and the pursuit of Happiness,"[62] then they belong to all mankind. If they belong to all mankind, then it is contrary to justice for King George III, or anyone else, not to ensure that all men have the right to life, the right to liberty, and the right to the pursuit of happiness.

Conclusion: Preemptive military action can be taken to establish the Tranquillitas Ordinis for the citizens of another place (notice that there may not be a recognizable nation in that place).

The Range of Preemptive Actions

ANTICIPATE: Anticipation is engagement with alliance nations in and around the location of interest. It is the conduct exercises and exchanges.

PREVENT: A nation can exercise prevention, but not in the old Europe style of preventively going to war to avoid an unbalancing of power.[63] Participate with alliance countries in active action against traffickers, insurgents, insurrectionists, for example. The other country has the lead, the US is the guest, but a participant.

INTERDICT: Interdiction is the task of providing ordinary tranquility. The responsibility to protect the tranquility "is in the first instance one of interdiction: preventing horrible things before they occur."[64] The idea that the Coast Guard and the Customs and Border Protection can stop things immediately at the border is an obsolete idea. Interdiction requires active pursuit, to include inside the borders of another country of those who would cause us harm. Interdiction is violence, but it is the "authorized violence of the guest" if international borders are crossed. Some categories of things that can be interdicted are: substances ("War on Drugs"); ideas; plans; electronic communications; and activities. Some interdicting activities will be intelligence activities, while others will be analogous to domestic police actions.

STRIKE: The strike will actually have a range of activities from a bombing or missile strike on a specific target to a building up of forces and an invasion. The key element of a strike is notification. In keeping with the Hague Conventions, notification will be given to the country where a target resides.

"Seek peace and pursue it"[65] is a motto of activity. Securing peace for its citizens is a primary responsibility of any nation. The words "secure the peace" provide the impetus for actively pursuing peace. In the pursuit of justice, seeking peace finds its focus. Preemptive actions are based on justice, but tempered by the considerations of Weinberger and Powell. If a nation cannot leave a place with "a more just peace"[66] then doing anything at all is illegitimate.

Section 7

Right Makes Right

Right intention is essential. As a matter of fact, *intent* is a fundamental aspect of law abiding societies. It is well known and understood that war is a messy activity, and that there are some unintended consequences of engaging in war. However, the purpose behind the participation governs whether or not the participation is proper. This denies that military might makes right.

The principles which will allow a nation to knowingly exercise its moral superiority for the good of its citizens and even for the good of the citizens of the world are the following:

1. Charity
2. Justice
3. Certain Unalienable Rights

That charity is the first principle for exercising power in any capacity for the good of citizens is addressed by Saint Ambrose (340-397 A.D.). He is considered the founder of the Western approach to war. For Ambrose, the two elements that dictate behavior in just war are "charity, which compels justice."[67] The requirement of charity is that citizens be of "mutual help to one another."[68]

Immediately following this key section on charity, Ambrose comments, "Great...is the glory of justice, for she exist[s]" for the good of others rather than self,[69] connecting the requirement of charity with the importance of justice. Saint Augustine (354-430 A.D.) continues the emphasis on justice. He calls kingdoms without justice "robberies."[70] The essential element, then, of civil society is justice. Therefore, justice ought to permeate the functions of government, including war.

The Declaration of Independence of the United States uses the phrase, "certain unalienable rights." The central idea which the founders captured in these words is that rights belong to individuals, and that the rights cannot be taken away from them. If they are taken away, the power that does so has violated its requirements of observing charity and carrying out justice. The application of this central idea is universal—those rights belong to "all men."[71]

It was the principles of the founding documents of the United States of America that were attacked on September 11, 2001, and which continue to be under pressure from terrorists. These principles are the ones that distinguish the US among the nations of the world. However, that does not mean that no other nation can be guided by the same principles, nor does it mean that no other nation is guided by them.[72] Rather, the pursuit of justice requires that we recognize the citizens of the world as joint owners of these fundamental rights.

The motto which defines this section is *"Do the Right thing; for the Right Reason; at the Right Time."* All preemptive actions must be guided by justice, informed by charity with equal regard for all mankind.[73]

Section 8

The Democratic Dilemma

The democratic dilemma, very simply, is that the will of the majority determines morality. This is a problem of haughtiness. It is a belief that, "Because I am in agreement with the majority, therefore I am right. Because the majority has concluded something it must be right." The extreme danger is that majorities have been known to be very wrong. It is for this reason, that there are such active provisions for the protection of the minority in our system of

23

government, including the assumption of "innocent until proven guilty."[74] The US Constitution does not actually use these words, but it is generally understood from the 5th, 6th and 14th Amendments, as well from the Writ of Habeas Corpus, which protects the right to a fair trial.

What is at stake here is the very substance of justice. Majority rule cannot actually dictate what is right, what is wrong, what is proper, what is good, or what is just, simply because a majority decreed it. Majority rule is often used to help evaluate between options, including the election of heads-of-state, and in a democracy, the deliberative value of the electoral process is trusted to reach the best conclusion. But these evaluations are not ones of justice, they are evaluations between options, any of which must be obliged to carry out justice. Therefore, the desire of a people who long for war, does not make the war that it seeks a just one. Rather, the Head of State is obligated to pursue justice under all circumstances.

The democratic dilemma does not necessarily have any relation to the actual might of a people. It is possible that a small or weak democracy could choose to engage in a war that may be unjust and a losing endeavor. Or, it could choose, by popular demand, to engage in a just war that is a losing endeavor.

Equally, might does not mandate justice. A mighty power can engage in a just war and fail, or succeed—democratically. If it has the "might" and the public's approval, winning a war is a likely outcome. Winning that conflict would not define the justness of the war, nor would losing define the incorrectness of the conflict.

Here an important principle emerges: *One cannot aid all*. One person cannot help all people; one nation cannot help all nations. Since "all men are to be loved equally, but you...cannot do good to all you are to pay special regard to those who...happen for the time being to be more closely connected with you."[75] Since all ought to be aided, but not all can be aided effectively, a just nation must aid those it can with the same considerations given to achieving a better peace. If aid of any type will not make a place better, then it ought not to be aided.

A just nation must desire justice for all mankind, but affect change for justice where it can be effective. From this, a better principle would state: *One cannot aid all; but one must aid all one can.* This is the best point for Weinberger's "national interest" to inform a decision about war. If national interest is left to its own devices, greed and expediency will rule the day. If, however, national interest is *tranquillitas ordinis* and justice for all mankind, then the pragmatism of Weinberger and Powell will inform a democratically elected president to make just choices about where and how those choices can accomplish justice for citizens of the world.

Conclusion

War, and the conduct of war, is a fundamental, moral, human endeavor that is based on ultimate questions. The Western Just War Tradition developed through the course of history from a particular religious and moral heritage to become a dominant thought process influencing war in the West. It is not specifically legislated as a national doctrine, but many of its parts carry the force of international law, and guide debate about war in western nations.

The dilemma studied in this work is whether or not the pursuit of justice can include the first use of military might. As its name implies, the Just War Tradition is concerned with justice. To the extent that any nation seeks justice, the JWT effectively informs the actions of that nation regarding warfare. The JWT also provides the moral framework for preemptive actions.

The National Security Strategy of 2002 is the opening salvo in what ought to be a real debate among the nations of the world about preemption. Operation Iraqi Freedom is not the opening salvo. OIF does not offer the test case for preemptive war, or whether preemptive war is allowable on the world scene due to its continuity with the First Gulf War and subsequent military actions in the region.

The Western world should rest assured that its JWT remains applicable today. Though the "world today" is in a state of confusion about how to think and what to do about extremists, jihadists, terrorists, rogue states and non-state actors, justice must be pursued by every nation.

The Just War Tradition does illumine preemptive actions, including preemptive war. It does more than shed light on the subject; it dictates how preemptive actions should be undertaken.

APPENDIX A

The National Security Strategy of the United States of America, 2002 (excerpt from page 15)

For centuries, international law recognized that nations need not suffer an attack before they can lawfully take action to defend themselves against forces that present an imminent danger of attack. Legal scholars and international jurists often conditioned the legitimacy of preemption on the existence of an imminent threat—most often a visible mobilization of armies, navies, and air forces preparing to attack.

We must adapt the concept of imminent threat to the capabilities and objectives of today's adversaries. Rogue states and terrorists do not seek to attack us using conventional means. They know such attacks would fail. Instead, they rely on acts of terror and, potentially, the use of weapons of mass destruction—weapons that can be easily concealed, delivered covertly, and used without warning.

The targets of these attacks are our military forces and our civilian population, in direct violation of one of the principal norms of the law of warfare. As was demonstrated by the losses on September 11, 2001, mass civilian casualties is the specific objective of terrorists and these losses would be exponentially more severe if terrorists acquired and used weapons of mass destruction.

The United States has long maintained the option of preemptive actions to counter a sufficient threat to our national security. The greater the threat, the greater is the risk of inaction— and the more compelling the case for taking anticipatory action to defend ourselves, even if uncertainty remains as to the time and place of the enemy's attack. To forestall or prevent such hostile acts by our adversaries, the United States will, if necessary, act preemptively.

The United States will not use force in all cases to preempt emerging threats, nor should nations use preemption as a pretext for aggression. Yet in an age where the enemies of civilization openly and actively seek the world's most destructive technologies, the United States cannot remain idle while dangers gather."

ENDNOTES

[1]Hillary Clinton, "Hillary Clinton: No Regret on Iraq Vote" Wednesday, April 21, 2004 at: http://www.cnn.com/2004/ALLPOLITICS/04/21/iraq.hillary [accessed Feb 19, 2008/2140]. Senator Clinton said she is not sorry she voted for a resolution authorizing President Bush to take military action in Iraq despite the recent problems there but she does regret "the way the President used the authority."

[2]International Committee of the Red Cross, http://www.icrc.org/ihl.nsf/CONVPRES?OpenView, accessed Feb 19, 2008.

[3]Alexander F.C. Webster and Darrell Cole. The Virtue of War: Reclaiming the Classic Christian Traditions East and West (Maryland: Regina Orthodox Press Inc, 2004), 51.

[4]Hugo Grotius, On the Law of War and Peace (Kitchener, Ontario: Batoche Books, 2001), 62.

[5]UNC Ch VII Article 51, http://www.un.org/aboutun/charter/chapter7.htm, accessed 7 March 2008.

[6]UNC ch 6 and 7 (all UNC chapters and articles can be accessed at: http://www.un.org/aboutun/charter/ via the navigation links on the left side of the screen).

[7]Long, Edward LeRoy, Jr, War and Conscience in America (Pennsylvania: Westminster Press, 1968), 27.

[8]Elshtain, Jean Bethke, Just War Against Terror: The Burden of American Power in a Violent World (New York: Basic Books, 2003), 57.

[9]Long, War and Conscience, 28.

[10]Convention with Respect to the Laws and Customs of War on Land (Hague II) (29 July 1899), http://www.yale.edu/lawweb/avalon/lawofwar/hague02.htm, accessed 19 Feb 2008, Article 26.

[11]Elshtain, Just War, 59.

[12]Long, War and Conscience, 27.

[13]Walzer, Michael. Just and Unjust Wars: A Moral Argument with Historical Illustrations. (New York: Basic Books, 1977), 110.

[14]Colin Powell, Foreign Affairs, Winter 1992, "US Forces: Challenges Ahead," http://www.pbs.org/wgbh/frontine1/shows/military/force/powell.html, accessed 24 Feb 2008.

[15]Gary Hess, <u>Presidential Decisions for War: Korea, Vietnam, and the Persian Gulf</u> (Baltimore: The Johns Hopkins University Press, 2001), 1. President Woodrow Wilson said, "One of the greatest of the President's powers is his control, which is very absolute, of the foreign relations of the nation." If the President is wielding national power in the nation's foreign relations, military power is only one of the strategic communication tools.

[16]Caspar Weinberger, "THE USES OF MILITARY POWER" Remarks prepared for delivery by the Hon. Caspar W. Weinberger, Secretary of Defense, to the National Press Club, Washington, D.C. Wednesday November 28, 1984. Transcript at: http://www.pbs.org/wgbh/pages/frontline/shows/military/force/weinberger.html, accessed 21 August 2007.

[17]Webster and Cole, <u>Virtue</u>, 51.

[18]Weinberger, Press Club.

[19]Powell, *Foreign Policy*.

[20]Grotius, <u>War and Peace</u>, 240.

[21]Walzer, <u>Just and Unjust</u>, 110. I have extended Walzer's statement that a just war assumes that there are purposes for which a soldier's life is "not too high a price."

[22]Long, <u>War and Conscience</u>, 27. Also see Ramsey, <u>Christian Conscience</u>, 30. Saint Augustine has the foundation of the notion of restoring the peace in <u>City of God</u>, Book XIX, ch. 12.

[23]Walzer, <u>Just and Unjust</u>, 123.

[24]Elshtain, <u>Just War</u>, 65.

[25]Hague II, Article 3.

[26]Geneva Conventions, Chapter I, Article 3.

[27]Webster and Cole, <u>Virtue</u>, 146.

[28]Elshtain, <u>Just War</u>, 66.

[29]Walzer, <u>Just and Unjust</u>, 8.

[30]Hague II, Article 23. Also see Hague IV (at Yale's Avalon Project) for information about balloons, something which is seemingly obsolete, but whose principle, i.e., accuracy, is still valid.

[31]Elshtain, <u>Just War</u>, 57-58.

[32]Long, <u>War and Conscience</u>, 24.

[33]Ibid., 29.

[34]Susan Niditch, <u>War in the Hebrew Bible: A Study in the Ethics of Violence</u> (New York: Oxford University Press, 1993), 12.

[35]Paul Ramsey, <u>War and the Christian Conscience: How Shall Modern War be Conducted Justly?</u>, (London, Cambridge University Press, 1961), 9.

[36]Ibid., 10.

[37]My purpose in the illustration is to show the tension among the parts of the Just War Tradition. In the illustration, I am not endorsing the selection of either course of action—to bomb, or not to bomb. Here is my selection: I do not think the bombings of Hiroshima and Nagasaki were justifiable. I could not have delivered the weapon. I wish my country could take back the grievous error. But it cannot be undone except by right action in the future. A national sense of guilt (if there is one) must not prevent just wars from being fought justly in the future.

[38]Walzer, <u>Just and Unjust</u>, 20.

[39]Webster and Cole, <u>Virtue</u>, 35.

[40]Ibid., 216.

[41]Weinberger, Press Club.

[42]Clausewitz, <u>On War</u>, 90.

[43] Declaration of Independence of the United States of America.

[44]George W. Bush. In regard to Afghanistan: Address to the Nation. Nov 8, 2001. In regard to Iraq: Radio Address, Mar 22, 2003.

[45]Weinberger, Press Club.

[46]Ibid. In addition to Weinberger's point about popular and Congressional support, he acknowledged that a candid Department of Defense would be necessary in order to maintain that support.

[47]Powell, Foreign Policy.

[48]Ibid.

[49]Clausewitz, <u>On War</u>, 605.

[50]Bush, speech. Remarks on Iraq, Cincinnati. October 7, 2002. Additionally, the House and Senate used JWT argumentation in Joint Resolution (H.J. Res. 114), which was passed as Public Law 107-243 of the 107th Congress on Oct. 16, 2002. It is available as a .pdf at: http://frwebgate.access.gpo.gov/cgi-bin/getdoc.cgi?dbname=107_cong_public_laws&docid=f:publ243.107.pdf

[51]Ibid. President Bush said, "Iraq possesses ballistic missiles with a likely range of hundreds of miles—far enough to strike Saudi Arabia, Israel, Turkey, and other nations—in a region where more than 135,000 American civilians and service members live and work. We've also discovered through intelligence that Iraq has a growing fleet of manned and unmanned aerial vehicles that could be used to disperse chemical or biological weapons across broad areas. We're concerned that Iraq is exploring ways of using these UAVS for missions targeting the United States. And, of course, sophisticated delivery systems aren't required for a chemical or biological attack; all that might be required are a small container and one terrorist or Iraqi intelligence operative to deliver it."

[52]Bush, speech. Radio Address to the Nation. October 5, 2002. In it he says, "Should force be required to bring Saddam to account, the United States will work with other nations to help the Iraqi people rebuild and form a just government. We have no quarrel with the Iraqi people."

[53]Clausewitz, On War, 221.

[54]The National Security Strategy of the United States, 2002, 15.

[55]Ibid., 15.

[56]Walzer, Just and Unjust, 110.

[57]Hebrews 10:28.

[58]Walzer, Just and Unjust, 74.

[59]Ibid., 81.

[60]Elshtain, Just War, 46.

[61]Long, War and Conscience, 26.

[62]Declaration of Independence of the United States of America.

[63]Walzer, Just and Unjust, 76-77.

[64]Elshtain, Just War, 49.

[65]Psalm 34:14.

[66]Aurelius Augustinus (St. Augustin), City of God, in Nicene and Post-Nicene Fathers, ed. Philip Schaff (Massachussetts: Hendrickson, 2004), 407.

[67]Webster and Cole, Virtue, 123.

[68]Saint Ambrose, Bishop of Milan, On the Duties of the Clergy, in Nicene and Post-Nicene Fathers, ed. Philip Schaff (Massachusetts: Hendrickson, 2004), Book I, Chapter XXVIII.135, 23.

[69]Ibid., Duties, Book I, Chapter XXVIII.136, 23.

[70]Augustine, City of God, 66.

[71]Elshtain, Just War, 59. She says, "Love of our neighbor—in this case, the Afghan people—is implicated as well. Or, less theologically, one could speak of equal regard for others based on human dignity and our common humanity." It is the idea of "equal regard for others" that is essential to the argument about Unalienable Rights belonging to all human beings. Furthermore, equal regard requires action on the part of each other individual human.

[72]Ibid., 27-28.

[73]Ibid., 28. See also Ramsey, Christian Conscience, 24, where he says, "The common assumption of Graeco-Roman political theory [is] that justice is the ethical substance of a commonwealth."

[74]The Universal Declaration of Human Rights. Article 11 says, "Everyone...has the right to be presumed innocent until proven guilty." While the US Constitution does not use this phrase, it is generally understood from the 5th, 6th and 14th Amendments, as well from the Writ of Habeas Corpus, which protects the right to a fair trial.

[75]Augustine, On Christian Doctrine, Book I Ch 28.29, 530.

BIBLIOGRAPHY

Ambrose, Saint, Bishop of Milan. On the Duties of the Clergy. In Nicene and Post-Nicene Fathers. ed. Philip Schaff. Massachusetts: Hendrickson, 2004.

Augustinus, Aurelius (St. Augustin). Confessions. In Nicene and Post-Nicene Fathers, ed. Philip Schaff. Massachussetts: Hendrickson, 2004.

Augustinus, Aurelius (St. Augustin). City of God. In Nicene and Post-Nicene Fathers, ed. Philip Schaff. Massachusetts: Hendrickson, 2004.

Augustinus, Aurelius (St. Augustin). On Christian Doctrine. In Nicene and Post-Nicene Fathers, ed. Philip Schaff. Massachusetts: Hendrickson, 2004.

Bush, President George W. Address to the Nation, World Congress Center. Atlanta, Georgia, November 08, 2001. http://www.whitehouse.gov/news/releases/2001/11/20011108-13.html (accessed 24 Feb 2008).

Bush, President George W. President Discusses Beginning of Operation Iraqi Freedom. President's Radio Address. March 22, 2003. http://www.whitehouse.gov/news/releases/2003/03/20030322.html (accessed 24 Feb 2008).

Bush, President George W. Radio Address to the Nation. October 5, 2002. http://www.whitehouse.gov/news/releases/2002/10/20021005.html (accessed 13 March 2008).

Bush, President George W. Remarks on Iraq. Cincinnati Museum Center - Cincinnati Union Terminal, Ohio. October 7, 2002. http://www.whitehouse.gov/news/releases/2002/10/20021007-8.html (accessed 13 March 2008).

Clausewitz, Carl Von. On War. Edited and Translated by Michael Howard and Peter Paret. New Jersey: Princeton University Press, 1976. Index 1984.

_____. Convention with Respect to the Laws and Customs of War on Land (Hague II) (29 July 1899). http://www.yale.edu/lawweb/avalon/lawofwar/hague02.htm (accessed 19 Feb 2008).

Elshtain, Jean Bethke. Just War Against Terror: The Burden of American Power in a Violent World. New York: Basic Books, 2003.

Grotius, Hugo. On the Law of War and Peace. Kitchener, Ontario: Batoche Books, 2001. Accessed via .pdf format.

Hess, Gary R. Presidential Decisions for War: Korea, Vietnam, and the Persian Gulf. Maryland: Johns Hopkins University Press, 2001.

Long, Edward LeRoy, Jr, War and Conscience in America. Pennsylvania: Westminster Press, 1968.

_____. *The National Security Strategy of the United States of America.* Washington, D.C.: The White House, September 2002. The NSS in pdf format is at: http://www.whitehouse.gov/nsc/nss.pdf (accessed 24 Feb 2008).

Niditch, Susan. War in the Hebrew Bible: A Study in the Ethics of Violence. New York: Oxford University Press, 1993.

Powell, Colin. "US Forces: Challenges Ahead." Foreign Affairs. Winter 1992. http://www.pbs.org/wgbh/frontline/shows/military/force/powell.html (accessed 24 Feb 2008).

Ramsey, Paul. War and the Christian Conscience: How Shall Modern War be Conducted Justly?, London, Cambridge University Press, 1961.

Reston, James, Jr. Dogs of God: Columbus, the Inquisition, and the Defeat of the Moors. New York: Doubleday, 2005.

_____. *The Universal Declaration of Human Rights.* United Nations. http://www.un.org/Overview/rights.html (accessed 16 March 2008).

Walzer, Michael. Just and Unjust Wars: A Moral Argument with Historical Illustrations. New York: Basic Books, 1977.

Webster, Alexander F.C. and Darrell Cole. The Virtue of War: Reclaiming the Classic Christian Traditions East and West. Maryland: Regina Orthodox Press Inc, 2004.

Weinberger, Caspar, "The Uses of Military Power" Remarks prepared for delivery by the Hon. Caspar W. Weinberger, Secretary of Defense, to the National Press Club, Washington, D.C. Wednesday November 28, 1984. Transcript at: http://www.pbs.org/wgbh/pages/frontline/shows/military/force/weinberger.html (accessed 21 August 2007).

www.ingramcontent.com/pod-product-compliance
Lightning Source LLC
Chambersburg PA
CBHW080733290526
45790CB00008B/3171